Higher Thoughts

WESLEY SCOTT

WESTBOW
PRESS
A DIVISION OF THOMAS NELSON

WestBow Press books may be ordered through booksellers or by contacting:

WestBow Press
A Division of Thomas Nelson
1663 Liberty Drive
Bloomington, IN 47403
www.westbowpress.com
1-(866) 928-1240

ISBN: 978-1-4497-6400-5 (sc)
ISBN: 978-1-4497-6399-2 (e)
ISBN: 978-1-4497-6398-5 (hc)

Library of Congress Control Number: 2012915174

Printed in the United States of America

WestBow Press rev. date: 08/31/2012

This book is dedicated in loving memory
of my son, Michael W. Scott

Table of Contents

Abraham's Testing

With a heavy heart, Abraham approached the mountain
With his promised son, Isaac, walking by his side;
The one so long awaited for by God's servant, Abraham,
The only son of Sarah, Abraham's beloved bride.

Tears ran down his leathered, old face,
And his heart felt like it would break in two;
Yet steadily he strode onward to the mountain,
Not understanding what God had asked him to do.

They gathered rock with which they built an altar,
With Isaac wondering what the sacrifice would be;
Abraham bound Isaac and laid him on the altar;
Then Isaac realized, *This sacrifice is to be me.*

With his knife held high, Abraham cried out,
"Above all, oh my God, may Thy will be done;
I will follow you to the ends of the earth,
Even if it means the life of my beloved son."

"Wait," came the cry from the Lord on high;
"I have provided a lamb to sacrifice instead;
I had to know the depth of your love
And your commitment to follow wherever I led."

Unspeakable joy filled old Abraham's heart
When he heard the words of the Lord;
He had passed the test, and now he could keep
The son promised by God that he and Sarah adored.

God repeated the promises He made so long ago,
Bringing peace to Abraham's heart and joy to his soul;
Now he most truly would follow God's Word,
And following God would be his highest goal.

Higher Thoughts

Affirmation

When despair happens to enter your mind,
Here are some words to enlighten your day;
Remember, deep from within your heart,
That discouragement really can go away.

I know I belong to the Father;
I know that He is mine;
I know that I am of His fruit,
And that I am growing on the vine.

He is the strength that is within me,
And through Him I can overcome any test;
Because the Lord I serve is a winner,
He always gives me His very best.

I am His ambassador here on earth,
And it is in Him whom I put my trust;
He placed His light within me to shine,
And shine through me I know it must.

I believe from the very depths of my heart,
And I have faith in what He can do;
He is the anchor I have in this life;
I will trust Him like He wants me to.

Wesley Scott

Afraid to Try?

Afraid to fail? Afraid to try?
Afraid to stretch your wings and fly?
If freedom lies but a few steps away,
If you're afraid to try, that's where it'll stay.

In this body that God has given
Lie many talents that have not yet risen;
Do you want them to wither and fade away
Like the old flowers of yesterday?

Learn by mistakes, we all must do,
But don't let them get the best of you;
Be not afraid of what others may say,
If a failure should happen to dampen your way.

Hold in your heart no fear to fail,
And be determined that you will prevail;
There is a power within your life
That is far above all earthly strife.

Let us call upon that power today,
And ask Him to cast all fears away;
Jesus is our power that lives inside;
When we call on Him, fear will subside.

All Because of You

Because of you, my life is so much brighter;
You are the sun that chased the clouds away;
You caused my heart to beat a little faster;
You are the reason for the love I feel today.

The beauty of your eyes is so alluring;
When you look at me, my heart melts away;
Your smile always lifts me higher;
My mind is fixed on every word you say.

Every time you touch me, it's like heaven;
You put my mind in the realm of ecstasy;
If this is but a dream, I pray I will not awaken,
Because this is how I want my life to be.

The love within my heart grows so much deeper
With the passing of each day that's born anew;
Your love is like a fire that consumes me,
And my life is now complete - all because of you.

Wesley Scott

Angels of Mercy

There are angels of mercy among us;
I know in my heart this is true;
They dedicate their lives to caring for others;
Out of compassion, they do what they do.

They stand ready to serve in an instant,
Whether that time be of day or of night;
It is for our comfort which they labor,
Always interested in doing what is right.

They have answered the call of their spirit,
Which was their heavenly call from above;
I feel God in His goodness does bless them,
Smothering them with His continual love.

Nurses in the title that behold them,
Beautiful of heart, they surely must be;
They bring comfort and aid to the sick;
Yes, nurses are angels of mercy to me.

Anger to Forgiveness

First the anger, then the sorrow;
It usually happens that way;
When the argument with another
Is lodged in my heart all day.

The feeling of forgiveness is wonderful,
But forgive - how can I forgive this day?
Yet the anger I hold will only bear fruit,
Unless it is cast very far away.

Cleanse my heart, I pray to You, Lord,
Oh, please take my anger away;
Replace it with love You give so freely,
Love that is offered anew each day.

Cause my heart to overrun with goodness;
Fill me, oh Lord, through and through,
Until the flower of forgiveness blooms inside
And my anger I can freely surrender to You.

Help me to forgive without holding on
To the feelings that once were so strong;
Fill me with the peace only You can give
As You forgive me, oh Lord, of my wrong.

Wesley Scott

Another Day

Life is a wonderful blessing
That God gives to us each day;
Another chance to show our love
While walking in His way.

Another opportunity to speak of Him
To someone who may not have heard;
Another day to live closer yet
Within His holy Word.

So, when the sun rises again
And God gives us another day,
It's a chance to show we are willing
To gladly go that way.

Another day to honor Him
By doing everything in love;
Another day to draw closer yet
To our heavenly Father above.

Another Year's Blessings

God has laid out another year before us
On this ladder of life that we climb;
We can master it the same way as the last,
Simply by taking it one step at a time.

He has set this year out as a blessing,
As He has set out many more before;
Let us beware or perhaps we will miss
All the opportunities He has placed in store.

As we enter into this brand new year,
Let trusting be the main endeavor we know;
Hope should reign supreme in our hearts
As we put faith in our ability to grow.

We should prepare for this year ahead
And condition our hearts from within,
Let's seek to rid ourselves of all negative feelings,
So that unencumbered, we may enter in.

As we thank God for the new year He gives
And for the blessings He gave for the last,
Then surely the promises this year does hold
Will be as great as the blessings of the past.

Wesley Scott

Appreciation

How often we take for granted
The things that other people do,
Often forgetting to respond
With simple words of "thank you."

Calloused, cold and conditioned
Can easily become our heart;
So involved in the things of the world,
Each trying to live up to his part.

Sometimes we should stop for a moment,
For super-humans not are we;
Let's give thanks for those God has given us
To help our lives more pleasant to be.

It's nice to know we are appreciated,
And a "thank you" goes a long way
Towards encouraging the life of someone else,
And it brightens up their day.

If we are to be beneficial to others,
Then more courteous we should all be;
And more appreciative of things others do
To help enrich the lives of you and me.

Armor of God

I thank Thee, dear Lord, for the armor Thou has given
With which I can resist the enemy today;
To stand firm in Thy truth and through Thy strength,
I shall be victorious in all that I do or say.

Thou has girded my loins with Thy truth,
So that nakedness I will never feel;
Your righteousness is the breastplate I wear,
Protected from Satan, which he can never steal.

My feet are fully shod in Thy Word,
And there shall be peace wherever I go;
The shield Thou has given is filled with my faith,
And the sting of enemy arrows I will not know.

The helmet of salvation placed on my head
Keeps doubts from entering my mind;
My sword is Thy truth, which bringeth new life
And which does strike the enemy blind.

Thy spirit Thou has placed inside of me
Does guide me and show me the way;
Now truly I am dressed in Thy armor,
Ready and willing to face each new day.

For Thine is the strength that sustains me;
By Thy blood, I have been set free;
Gladly will I serve you, oh Lord,
As I realize more fully Thy deep love for me.

Wesley Scott

Ask, Seek and Knock

Ask, and you shall receive; seek, and you will find;
Knock, and it shall be opened unto you;
These are the words of our precious Lord Jesus
In chapter seven, verse seven in the book of Matthew.

What a wonderful promise to look forward to;
What a joyful reality to live in day by day;
There are no disappointments for those who believe in Jesus,
The confirmation in Romans ten, verse eleven does say.

Anyone who calls upon the name of the Lord Jesus,
Surely He shall hear, and they shall be saved;
What a wonderful, sweet, caring Savior we have,
Who does save us from a world that is sick and depraved.

Let us then knock, and the door shall be opened;
Let us then seek, and surely we will find,
The more faith we place in our dear Lord Jesus,
The more the cares of the world can be left behind.

Attaining Faith

With faith, we can unlock a brand-new world,
Which otherwise in our lives we never will see;
Within our minds and deep in our hearts,
There alone in each of us does lie the key.

In faith, we can take what He promised,
That which we are to claim as our own;
If indeed there is faith deep in our hearts,
Faith in our Savior, and in Him all alone.

How often Jesus did speak of this faith
And did tell of what a mighty thing it could be;
Of how it can bring fulfillment into our lives
And shape them more as He would have them to be.

By our faith, we are saved through grace;
However, faith must be the first to enter in;
Because only by having faith in our hearts,
Can Jesus' precious blood cleanse our sin.

All things are possible if you have faith,
Jesus says so plainly in Mark nine, twenty-three;
Yes, anything we request, asking in His name,
Jesus says it shall be done for you and me.

Then doubt should not enter into our mind,
And in our faith, we can reach out and receive
The blessing He himself has promised,
Because we, as His children, do truly believe.

Wesley Scott

Attitude

Our attitudes can short circuit our faith,
Limiting us in what God calls us to do,
Erecting a barrier within our lives
That keeps us from enjoying faith born anew.

There is no such thing as a nobody;
We all have talents and power within;
It is up to us to bring them forth,
And now is the best time to begin.

We live in the presence of the eternal now;
The past is dead and the future not here;
So, let's burst forth in a leap of faith,
Overcoming all obstacles based on fear.

Place your trust in God, and take His hand;
Have faith in your heart He's there;
He will lift you above all wrong attitudes,
As you submit yourself into His care.

Backside of the Mountain

When we help someone in need,
Just where is it that we stand?
On the backside of the mountain,
Or with an audience close at hand?

God sees everything we do,
No mountains can stand in His way;
He knows our hearts, our minds, our thoughts,
The reasons we do what we do each day.

Everything we possess belongs to God;
His seeds of goodness, He wants us to sow,
On the backside of the mountain,
Where only you and God will know.

Let us not seek to be pleasers of men;
All things are temporary that we see;
Instead, let us give thanks to God,
Whose rewards will last throughout eternity.

Wesley Scott

Be My Valentine

Your hands have the touch of an angel;
Your lips are sweeter than the fresh morning dew;
Tell me, how in the world could I ever be
Anything but in love with you?

When you hold me, my heart starts to pound;
My mind slips into a sweet ecstasy;
The song that my spirit is singing,
Is that you will always be the one for me.

Through the years, my love has grown deeper,
And I feel in my heart we are one,
Bound together by an inseparable tie;
What a wonderful thing love has done.

Since Valentine's Day is special for lovers,
And you have put me up on cloud nine,
Please, oh my darling, won't you promise me
That you will always be my Valentine.

Beauty and Love

The world is full of beauty
When our hearts are full of love;
That's when we see the best in all things,
As does our heavenly Father above.

The beauty that always surrounds us
Is abundant in this life that we live,
In everything that God did make,
And in the amazing friends he did give.

God has blessed us in so many ways;
His love in us does always abound;
As we drink of His cup of kindness,
Our deepest fulfillment in life is found.

When His spirit does sing within us,
Surging and swelling within our chest,
It brings us into a new awareness
That life most truly is at its best.

Wesley Scott

Believe to Receive

Jesus came to restore the will of the Father
Because of the sin that had entered in;
When Jesus died for us, His mission was fulfilled;
He paid for our sickness, as well as our sin.

If you believe within your heart
The Word of God is undeniably true,
Then you must also believe and confess
The healing Jesus paid for was meant for you.

Since His will is undisputedly the basis of our faith,
His Word does so very plainly say,
Whatever we ask in the name of Jesus,
He will give it to us when we pray.

We only have to believe in order to receive
The healing that comes in His name;
We serve a God who only wants our good,
And He is always and forever the same.

Best Wishes

May you drink fully from His cup of kindness;
May the blessings He gives continually overflow;
May He enrich the lives of those around you,
As you plant the good seeds He gives to sow.

May words of faith come from your tongue
With more power day after day;
May He bless you with His almighty hand
And keep all earthly troubles far away.

May His spirit of wisdom dwell in your mind
And your understanding grow deeper each day;
May you follow the path He has set before you,
As you depend on Him each step of the way.

May your eyes continually search for the good
In others you become privileged to know;
May the seeds you plant find fertile ground,
Where the light of God will cause them to grow.

May Christ always remain the king of your heart,
As you put Him first in everything you do;
May your life on earth bring forth good fruits,
And may there be golden crowns waiting for you.

Wesley Scott

Between the Lines

Sometimes when letters are written,
There are so many things they do not say;
Unless you read between the lines,
The true feelings might just slip away.

Much is written between the lines
That only the eyes of your heart can see,
Feelings that cannot be expressed
As adequately as they really should be.

Feelings of love and feelings of affection
Can only come from our heart within;
They are from our higher nature
That our heart is embedded in.

Words can paint a beautiful picture
For us to see within our mind;
When connected with the thread of love,
Reality, they will one day find.

Feelings of love that come from my heart
Are written for you between the lines;
Read them with your heart and not your eyes,
Then peace, comfort and love I hope you find.

Birthday Wishes

May you walk in the light of the sun,
As each day being the celebration of your birth;
May God fill your heart with overflowing love,
So you can be a real blessing to this earth.

May others sense the love He has placed in your heart
Through the good works He has you do;
May you remember wherever you go,
God's special love will always flow through you.

May your days be as endless in number
As the sand by a great and mighty sea;
May the constant prayer upon your lips
Be, "Thank you, dear Lord, for using me."

May you be like a star in the heavens
That will guide others along the way;
May these be the gifts God gives to you,
As He overflows your heart on your birthday.

Wesley Scott

Blessed Are They

Blessed are they who follow in My footsteps
And who do my Father's holy will;
They are truly the children of God,
For My commandments they willingly fulfill.

Truly blessed are they who seek after Me,
For I am eternal life's only true door;
In Me, you will find true peace of mind
And contentment in your heart forever more.

Though the way may be narrow, do not despair,
For eternity lies on the other side;
That which you give shall joyfully be returned,
Pressed down in abundance, and many times multiplied.

Your labor is not in vain, for the ending is near,
It is whispered by My spirit to your mind;
Prepare your hearts now, for I am coming soon,
And many faithful workers I want to find.

Keep always My Word tucked in your heart
And your lives in the work I would do;
For you are the true children of God,
And I will be coming shortly for you.

Blessings

Life is such a beautiful gift
God gives to us each day;
We can experience the many wonders
He humbly places our way.

Surely, He does bless our lives
With all the beauty that we see,
All the marvels He has placed around us
In this kingdom He caused to be.

There are so many ways He does bless us
Through friends that we have known;
How compassion fills our hearts
When their love to us they have shown.

How blessed are we when ones in need
Are placed within our way;
We can then gladly share the blessings
He gives to us each and every day.

From the sunrise to the sunset,
Continuing all through the night,
When we put our love and trust in Him,
We know everything will be all right.

Wesley Scott

The Broken Body

Must we argue among ourselves,
So caught up in earthly strife,
And wile away the precious time
God has given us in this life?

Can't we be of flexibility?
Must things always be our way?
Is it not foolish to split the hairs
About what God's Word does say?

Division has broken the body of Christ
Of which we are all a part;
Do you think this brings glory to Jesus,
Or do you think it saddens His heart?

Let's all lay our pettiness aside
And truly be of one accord;
We should all love one another
And worship Jesus Christ, our Lord.

Broken Heart

Don't look now, but your broken heart is showing,
And you know it doesn't look good on you;
You can't hide the way you are feeling;
It shows through no matter what you do.

When you took my heart and broke it
And turned around and walked away,
Leaving me for the sake of a new love,
I still feel that rejection yet today.

You probably know I've always loved you,
And I still feel the same way right now;
I imagined I'd like to see you hurting,
But it just makes me hurt more somehow.

You are the only one I've ever loved;
When I lost you, I thought I lost my heart;
So, won't you come back to me, my darling,
And we can make a brand-new start.

Wesley Scott

Call for the Righteous

We cannot hear the call for the righteous,
If our hearts are ladened with sin;
We cannot be one with the spirit,
If His pathway we are not walking in.

He calls us in love to believe and have faith;
He gives us the strength to succeed;
At all times when we turn to Him,
He is faithful to meet our every need.

We should cleave to His precious love
And offer all we have to Him in return;
We should follow the light He shines on our path,
The light of truth which forever will burn.

We are walking on the treads of time,
No one knows when the end will be;
Soon, He will call his children to heaven,
Saying, "Come now and spend eternity with Me."

The Candle

Learn a lesson from the burning candle,
With its flickering rays of light;
As long as it continues to burn,
It holds at bay the fingers of the night.

Shadows seek to consume it;
They surround it on every side;
They wait for the last flicker of light,
Which is now pushing darkness aside.

The candle is not afraid of the dark;
It's been the victor its whole life through;
It depends on the light from within,
Just as you and I must certainly do.

We must live in the light within us,
And take strength from the way it does shine;
It glows through us to a darkened world;
It can bring divine insight to eyes once blind.

Where it shines, darkness cannot hold it;
It consumes all blackness in its way;
As we let the light of God shine through,
More people it will reach every single day.

Wesley Scott

Captured by His Love

Jesus has captured my heart with His undying love,
  Which totally surrounds me both night and day;
    To Him, I have surrendered all that I am,
    The most willing of captives, I will always stay.

  Safe I now feel in the bondage of His love;
    It constantly encompasses everything I know;
    He is my strength and my wall of happiness,
    And total contentment is what I seek to show.

  I shall struggle not for my own freedom's sake,
    For, in Him, my true freedom I have found;
      I have yielded my heart fully unto Him,
      And I now dwell on His holy ground.

May the sentence I serve be forever unending,
    For true joy and happiness does it bring;
    Such contentment I now feel in my heart,
    It causes my spirit from within me to sing.

  It sings of His mercies, it sings of His love,
    It sings from the depths of my soul;
May I give glory to God, with praises unending;
  To honor only Him is my life's highest goal.

Centered in Life

Our hearts need to be in the right place
If we are ever going to get anywhere;
If they are not, then we are unbalanced,
And we are going to stay right there.

Are the thoughts on which our mind dwells
Of things which are good and true?
Or will they become like stumbling blocks
That in our life's path we grew?

If our lives are centered in Christ,
Our hearts will be centered too;
Then no more wandering to and fro
In this walk of life will we do.

We should walk the path He leads,
And hold Him firmly by the hand;
We will then know our lives are centered,
And our vision will be on the promised land.

Wesley Scott

Children

Children are a precious gift in our lives
That our heavenly Father does give;
They are to be nurtured, cuddled and loved
As a high responsibility in this life we live.

They are a wonderful part of the two
God lovingly joined together as one,
A replica to always remind us
Of Jesus, God's own beloved Son.

There must be a special angel watching,
So precious are they in His sight;
God trusts us so deep within His heart,
We should protect them both day and night.

Be thankful for the trust God places in us
In this wonderful gift of His love;
May their pathways be pleasing to the Lord,
As their true guidance comes from above.

Choices

Will you choose to give Jesus your life,
Or turn around and go the other way?
Will you accept the poisoned pill Satan offers
In this mixed-up world of today?

It does not work to serve two masters;
It only makes sense that you must choose;
And whichever one it is that wins,
The opposite one will surely lose.

He is our strength, He is our hope;
All good things come from His hand;
He will not live with the children of darkness,
For they will not dwell in His holy land.

Yes, there is a choice we all must make,
And each one must make His own;
Which master is it that we will serve -
The serpent or the Holy One on the throne?

Wesley Scott

Christ Has Risen

Glorious and triumphant, Christ has risen;
He has defeated death, our arch enemy;
He has broken the chains that once bound us;
He has opened the gates and set the captives free.

He is our Lord, he is our risen Savior;
May His name be praised now and evermore;
We have been joined as part of His kingdom;
All the broken bonds, Jesus did restore.

Easter is a special day to thank the Lord
For the marvelous things He did do;
He has opened up the doorway to heaven
To share His glorious victories with you.

Lift up your heart and give Him all praise;
Rejoice with songs the Spirit gives you;
Give thanks to Him, for He is always faithful;
Let us seek to honor Him in all we say and do.

He has given unto us His own eternal light,
And forever through our lives it should shine;
Christ is the light who shines through darkness;
He can shine through hearts like yours and mine.

Christmas Gift

This year give a gift for Christmas,
One that will bring much delight;
You don't even have to wrap it up
With ribbons all shiny and bright.

This gift will cause the angels to rejoice
And sing happily around God's throne;
But this gift can only be given,
Just by you and you alone.

You can give it right where you are;
It doesn't cost any money at all;
Jesus stands knocking at your heart,
All you need to do is answer His call.

Just say, "Jesus, I give You my heart,
Dear Lord, will You please come inside?"
Then, all the peace you will start to feel,
You couldn't describe it if you tried.

This Christmas won't you consider
Answering the Lord's loving call;
Decide to give your heart to Jesus,
It will be the most precious gift of all.

Wesley Scott

A Closer Walk

Seek yet a closer walk with Me,
And I will lift you higher still,
For it is then, My precious child,
You are more closely within My will.

I have set many desires within your heart,
Their fullness I would have you to know;
Come, my child, walk closely with Me,
It is My desire that you should grow.

Open up your whole heart to Me,
And lay all of your unbelief aside;
My Spirit can then come more fully in,
It will be your gentle, loving guide.

There is so much work I want to do
To shape you in the image of My Son;
Draw closer to me now, My child;
My work in you has just begun.

Come to Him

Come to Him when you are feeling weary
And the world is pulling you down;
He always accepts us just as we are,
And comfort in Him can forever be found.

"Come to Me you who are weary of heart,
And I shall give you rest,"
Is the soothing promise in the Bible
That comforts me perhaps the best.

In all our ways, we are not perfect;
We know in our hearts we never will be;
We can be happy to be just who we are,
For through Jesus, we have that liberty.

When we bring our troubles to the Lord,
And through prayer with Him we share,
He will lighten the burdens we carry,
For through His love, we are under His care.

Wesley Scott

Complete in Jesus

Just as though my sins had never happened,
So complete is God's forgiveness of me;
I stand before Him without spot or blemish;
His righteousness and grace, He does shed over me.

Jesus is the light that illuminates my soul;
His are the eyes where mine cannot see;
He straightens the pathway on which I travel;
In Him, I am as complete as I can possibly be.

He is the rock, the anchor of all ages,
The harbor where the peaceful waters lie;
When storms of life batter me about,
It is on Him I know I can always rely.

So great is His love He has for me,
He gave His own life so I could be free;
With wonderment, I now stand before Him,
And ask him what he desires from me.

Concentrate on Today

Let's worry much less about our tomorrows,
And be more concerned about what we do today;
Today is the reality in which we now live,
And tomorrow is still so far away.

We create what happens to us tomorrow
By actions we take and what we say and do;
Since this reigns true within our lives,
Should not today be most important to you?

Don't get overly concerned about tomorrow
And what destiny for us the next days do hold;
Believe in your heart that what you deserve
Will be there when the future does unfold.

God promises us not any of our tomorrows,
Yet He gives us the great gift of life today;
We should bask in the sunshine of His love,
And let Him lead us every step of the way.

Wesley Scott

Confessions of Faith

Confess with your mouth that Jesus is Lord;
Believe in your heart He was raised from the dead;
For by doing so, your soul will be saved,
In Romans 9:10, in God's Word, it is said.

When we believe, we cast aside all doubts
And allow our heart and mind to be free;
We set aside all the shackles of life,
So we can be faithful like He wants us to be.

He takes our fears far away from us,
So undaunted in His presence we can stand;
We can receive His grace in abundance,
Which He offers us with His outstretched hand.

Through Jesus, His Son, He has lifted us up,
Restored us to righteousness before His holy eyes;
He has given us the power to overcome all sin;
He loves us much more than we realize.

We are partakers in the nature of God;
If we follow His ways, we will not fail;
He is our strength and anchor in life,
The bright, burning light illuminating our trail.

Consideration

Be considerate of other people's mistakes,
As you have made many of them on your own;
Always treat each other with respect;
Otherwise, how can your love be shown?

Be forgiving and show compassion
For the wrongs others have done;
Don't be judgmental of others,
For you are not the perfect one.

Don't make others feel unimportant,
But be courteous in all that you do;
Only if you show respect for others,
Will that respect be shown back to you.

Let your heart be full of understanding;
Don't yell or raise your voice;
Speak forth all your words in love;
It really is your very best choice.

Be a candle of hope for others;
Lift them up in all that you say;
And God in all of His goodness
Will surely show you the way.

Wesley Scott

Correcting Properly

When we correct each other in anger,
It causes resentment to build inside;
Resentment uncalled for and unwanted,
I think we could do better if we tried.

When we correct each other in love
And understanding within our heart,
It opens the door to positive action,
And it doesn't push friends apart.

We are all learning in this world
And so many faults have we;
Yet, if we stop and think for a moment,
Very helpful to others we can be.

Let's try to be more understanding
When each other's faults we see;
Then we will be more in God's will,
And that's where He wants us to be.

Counselor's Prayer

You know, oh God, of my transgressions,
Yet no fault in me do you see;
Lord, help me to be as loving to others
As You have always been to me.

Help me to forgive all others
When wrong have been their ways;
Help me to only see their good
And pray for them for better days.

Help me when I admonish them,
I do it with love and concern in my heart;
For you, oh Lord, are judge over all,
And of judging let me have no part.

I want to strengthen and guide them
And nurture them in Your loving ways;
Let my hand reach out in understanding,
Oh Lord, to You, my heart prays.

Wesley Scott

Crying of the Trees

Save us from the clear cutting man
Is the desperate crying of the trees;
They seek to level us to the ground;
Won't you listen and help us please?

They have harvested our bounty for years,
But it was always with a kinder hand;
They thinned us out, but let us flourish,
And then along came the clear cutting man.

Let us stand so we may shade our young,
Lest the heat of the sun take them away;
One by one, they are destroying us;
How barren and wasted many forests do lay.

We have lived here together for generations;
We have shaded and protected this land;
Won't you help us in our desperate plight,
And save us from the clear cutting man?

Depending on Jesus

When we don't depend on Jesus,
It is often then that we fail;
For He alone supplies the strength
With which to meet our every travail.

He is in authority over Satan
And of all the evil spirits he commands;
He's made us children of the light,
No longer subject to Satan's demands.

He has given us the power of His name,
The name to which we can always turn;
It is through Him that we get our strength
And the wisdom through which we learn.

So let's open up our hearts to Jesus
And invite Him to come fully inside;
He will clean the chambers of our heart
Until there is nothing left to hide.

His power can then flow through us;
His authority will dwell in the words we say;
And, surely, as we become more like Jesus,
We will depend on Him more and more each day.

Wesley Scott

Desert Storm

Awesome is the power of God
As the desert storm draws near;
Thunder crashing through the sky,
It's startling to the ear.

The sky is turning darker now,
And it's rumbling deep within;
Streaks of lightning pierce the sky;
The show is about to begin.

Drops of water pounding down
Sent rushing through the air,
As though to cool the lightning bolts
Which are flashing everywhere.

"Rejoice with me," cries the rain,
Streaking through the air;
"God has sent me as a blessing
To this desert land so bare."

The powers of God are amazing;
No one can deny this to be;
He sends rain unto this land
So loved by you and me.

Desiring the Lord

He is our Lord, and He is our Savior;
In Him, we are all that we can ever be;
Filled to the fullest, with nothing left wanting,
Wrapped securely in His love for eternity.

How can we speak with words from our mouths
To describe the feelings we know deep inside?
They seek us, they find us, in love's spell they bind us;
They are in us so deeply, there is nothing to hide.

He lives in every fiber of this body He gave us;
He encourages us when our own strength is wane,
He never gives up, His love never fails us;
In Him, there's nothing to lose and all things to gain.

There is such a desire that dwells deep inside us;
We want to see him in all His glory and might;
Oh, what splendor when we will behold Him;
We will be blessed by such a wonderful sight.

His spirit fills us with such a warm feeling
And places a desire not of our own;
It is a gift from our heavenly Father,
A gift from Him - and Him all alone.

Wesley Scott

Different Gifts

Don't let anyone plant confusion in your mind
About the Holy Spirit and you,
Saying that you must speak in tongues,
Because you see not all of us do.

Not all of us have the same gifts,
The Bible does plainly say;
In First Corinthians 12 through 14,
It is written exactly that way.

The Bible teaches if we do speak in tongues,
It is to edify our holy God;
It is not to be used as a means to cause
Another person to feel down trod.

We are joined to His Holy Spirit
From the moment we first pray, *come in;*
From then on, Jesus speaks to our heart,
And His Holy Spirit dwells within.

Let us then not be misguided
By what others may sometimes say;
Don't doubt the dwelling of the Holy Spirit,
For His Spirit is in us, forever to stay.

Directions

Just like reading directions on a box
Will instruct in a proper way,
If you read the Word inspired by God,
You'll discover it has much to say.

It declares of the love God has for us
And the trials He has gone through
To prepare our hearts more like His,
So we can live the way He wants us to.

It tells of ways to fill our lives
With the blessings He does give,
If selfishness we will lay aside
And within His ways, we will live.

It reveals the gift of eternal life
And how it was given by his Son;
It speaks of the power of Jesus' name,
For He declares that They are one.

It tells of so many stories
Of the faithful who have gone before;
How their lives did bless this earth
And will bless it forever more.

God inspired them in their hearts
And caused them to write it down;
So, as long as there is a Bible on earth,
We shall know how true freedom is found.

The directions are written clearly,
So every reader may know the way;
If we ask Jesus into our hearts,
Eternally there, He promises to stay.

Wesley Scott

Disciple's Commitment

A disciple's commitment is the key to the kingdom;
It's a desire to live fully within God's will;
We should put Him first within our lives,
So that His plan for us we may fulfill.

We must not be captured by evil deceptions
Or false philosophy that is rampant today;
We have the truth that He has given us,
Which puts all thoughts of idolatry far away.

He is speaking to our hearts and opening our eyes
So, with spiritual eyes, our hearts can see
That constant relationship and growing closer to Him
Is the greatest fulfillment there can possibly be.

Let us surrender our lives and wrong attitudes,
Our disobedience, arguments and self-pretense today;
He has clothed us in His own righteousness;
He gives it for us to walk in day by day.

Don't Be Afraid to Cry

Once I was a hardened man,
For many years I had not cried;
All of the sorrow and hurt I felt,
I was conditioned to hold inside.

It is not manly to cry, I was told;
You should hide your tears all away;
Stand and take things on the chin,
It will make you a man someday.

If we suppress our feelings inside,
Though normal as they may be,
It causes a hardening in our hearts
When we fail to react naturally.

If you feel the need to cry
To release the emotions inside,
Don't be afraid to let the tears flow;
Feelings are something you need not hide.

Wesley Scott

Doorways of Life

One door closes, and another one opens,
And it always leads to a higher way;
The blessings on the other side
Will be ours to claim one day.

Life is but a growing experience,
If so perceived within our mind;
Welcome the door that opens,
And let the past then lie behind.

Let's gather our courage and our wits;
Step boldly through that door;
We should have faith within our heart
That only good does it hold in store.

If tempered steel is always tested
So that stronger it may be,
Then should it not also be true
In shaping the lives of you and me.

God gives us life so we may grow
And a mind so we may understand;
Welcome the opening of each door
As a blessing from His holy hand.

Higher Thoughts

Doubt and Fear

We, as humans, often wonder if God will keep His word,
Sometimes thinking maybe the Bible isn't even true;
The fear of failure stops our trust in God;
It hinders all the things He would have us do.

Fear is most always based on the unknown,
Yet through His eyes we can clearly see
By renewing our faith and trust in Him,
We can replace doubt and fear with victory.

God doesn't give us impossible tasks,
Only things He knows we can do;
We must crush the spirit of doubt and fear
With the power He gives to me and you.

Trust in God and have faith in His Word;
He is the sustainer of the life that we live;
He is the power, the light and the truth;
And everything we need, He will surely give.

Wesley Scott

Each Day

God gives life to me each day,
And I can do with it as I choose;
If I use it to bring honor to Him,
I know there is no way I can lose.

For when I honor him, my God,
And put Him the highest above all,
His blessings flow like living water;
He is always there to answer my call.

He is so faithful, He loves me so much;
The truth is in His holy name;
He never tires of doing good;
He is forever and always the same.

He loved me enough to give His only Son,
Asking simply that in Him, I believe;
I will then know the way to eternal life
Only through Jesus can I receive.

I shall honor Him with all of my life;
That is what I was put on earth for;
One day I know that He will answer
When I knock on His eternal door.

The Eagle

I see an eagle soaring
Far above its nest,
Landing in a crooked tree
Upon the mountain crest.

With awe I watch it fly,
So free and high above;
Yet, I feel a profound sorrow
For this magnificent bird I love.

One by one God's species
Seem to disappear from earth;
Once they are gone, never again
Shall they bring forth new birth.

I see the pollution from the city
Creeping across the valley floor;
Just how much can we pollute
Until we can stand no more?

Must we destroy all we touch,
Or don't we really care anymore?
I wonder if our children's children
Will ever see an eagle soar?

Wesley Scott

Easter

Jesus took the sins that once were ours
And claimed them as His own,
So we may be covered by His righteousness
As we stand before the Father's throne.

The bonds of death could hold Him not,
And on the third day He did rise;
Paid eternally, were the wages of sin,
Gone forever before God's holy eyes.

Now there is a light that is shining,
Brightly now that all may see;
Jesus is the light of God unto man;
The Savior who has set the captives free.

Rejoice, for the chains have been broken;
Jesus, our Redeemer, has set us free;
Everlasting life now belongs to us;
Jesus, the Victor, has won the victory.

Hallelujah, all praise be given to God;
May His name be lifted today;
Now millions have the chance to follow;
Thank you, Lord, for this glorious day.

Essence of Beauty

Fall in love with the person inside,
Not with the physical beauty they show;
For in the heart lies the true essence
Of every person we come to know.

Physical beauty is but for a season,
And in time, it will pass away;
The beauty that comes from within
Forever more, it continues to stay.

If our eyes are the mirrors of our soul,
As so many people claim them to be,
Let us all look deeper inside,
For real beauty there we can see.

Someday we will look in Jesus' eyes
And enraptured our hearts will be;
We'll be bound together with eternal love,
For the essence of all beauty is He.

Wesley Scott

Everlasting Grace

Everlasting grace is the gift God gives us;
It's a gift time cannot erode away;
Everlasting love is our inheritance,
When we ask Jesus into our heart to stay.

Everlasting through the annals of time,
And lasting through all eternity,
Is the wonderful grace He freely gives
To cover the lives of you and me.

There are no shadows in our path
Where His grace does fade away;
Once we are within His hand,
Forever there, we shall stay.

His is the grace that sustains us;
It is His power that has set us free;
He is the shepherd that tends to us;
We are His flock throughout eternity.

Everything

Everything we have has come from God;
He is the most magnificent provider of all;
If we will but seek His kingdom first,
Then, surely, we will answer His holy call.

As we live our lives and grow in faith,
He will be there to meet all our needs;
He will bless our lives with great abundance
As He multiplies our sowing seeds.

The blessings of life will follow our faith,
For when we serve Him, we labor not in vain;
Let the words 'all these things I will add unto you'
Echo many times over in our heart again.

As we live according to His Word,
We shall be victorious in all we do;
We can stand strong in our faith and belief in Him
And get to know Him better each day anew.

Wesley Scott

Faith

We should make faith the focal point of our lives,
For our faith determines how far we shall go;
Only through faith, can we reach out and claim
All of the promises God desires us to know.

By His stripes, we are healed from our sickness;
By His blood, we have been washed free from all sin;
One statement is not truer than the other,
For the same holy Bible, they are both written in.

Let nothing in our lives ever hold us back
From the victories that are ours to claim;
In God's holy Word, it is written,
We shall speak in the power of Jesus' name.

Lay hands on the sick, and they shall recover;
Pray a prayer of faith, and then let it be;
Wonderful, powerful, mighty promises,
Not yet fulfilled, but through faith soon to be.

When, within our hearts, we do believe
And accept all He gives us in every way,
We will grow ever nearer to His likeness,
As faith fills our heart much fuller each day.

The First Christmas

The world of darkness has been shattered
By our loving God's bright, shining light;
For, behold, the gift of His holy Son
Was given to us that first Christmas night.

The angels came down from heaven
To welcome in this new-born king;
They were overcome with joy, for they knew
It was our salvation that He did bring.

A special star did shine in the sky
To show the wise men the way;
It guided them to the baby Jesus,
So their homage they could pay.

The gift which was so long awaited
Arrived that first Christmas day;
Through that gift comes eternal light,
Which darkness can never take away.

The world has never been the same
Since Jesus was first sent to earth;
Let us lift our hands in praise to God,
And give joy with the angels for Jesus' birth.

Wesley Scott

Followers of Jesus

By these things, you shall know His followers;
They do the work which was started long ago;
They lay hands on the sick, and they recover;
They speak forth words of faith, and it is so.

He is the shepherd, the one they follow;
They seek neither the world nor its ways;
Their eyes are fixed on Jesus, their Savior,
And on Him, continually, is where it stays.

Let us find faith and trust in these words,
'For by faith, are we saved through grace',
All we do through Him, He will not forget
On that day we meet Him face to face.

All the works He has laid out before us,
Surely, He has given us the power to do;
When we reach out in faith and trust Him,
We are filled with wonderful abilities too.

We should make faith the guide in our lives,
And trust the promises He alone does give;
Let's be the good vessel our Lord can use,
So He can bless this world in which we live.

Gift of Life

The gift of life is a most precious gift
Our Father in heaven does give;
It's a chance to bring honor to Him
As we travel the path that we live.

Some are denied this gift of life
Through the decisions of others today;
Denied their right to live on earth
Because they might get in the way.

Children should be a joy in our lives;
Our heritage to all of mankind;
An integral part of two joined together;
The most precious gift one can find.

No one should be denied the gift of life,
For it is from God's own holy hand;
Each life is created expressly unique
To bring a special blessing in the land.

We must not destroy life God has given;
It is so very precious in His sight;
Abortion destroys the life of a child,
Do you believe in your heart, this is right?

Wesley Scott

Gift of Prayer

How sweet and how wonderful is the gift of prayer,
Which God, in His goodness, has caused there to be;
A way of us reaching the ear of our Father;
The gift of communication He gives to you and me.

How close it does cause us to feel to our Maker
When we offer Him prayer and praise from our heart;
In His great love, He lifts us even closer,
Through His spirit in us, who is an integral part.

If we give thanks always, and pray without ceasing,
How enraptured in love our hearts would then be;
The solitude of time is forever unending,
Holy Father, when we offer prayer unto Thee.

Your Word does say it is the sweet smelling incense,
Which reaches Your throne when to You we do pray;
May You continually be surrounded by this fragrance,
For we love you, dear God, in every possible way.

Girl in My Dreams

You are a bright ray of sunshine
On a cold and gloomy day;
With a sweet and loving smile,
You take all my dreariness away.

You are like a star in the sky,
That so very brightly does shine;
You hold me enraptured and spellbound,
And I am so glad that you are mine.

Your beauty is so much to behold;
It captivates and carries my heart away;
Just one loving look from you,
Sends my life into complete disarray.

My arms reach out to hold you,
But you always seem to slip away;
I am left feeling cold and empty
And unsure how to face another day.

Yet night time will again return,
And I am trusting you will too;
Oh, beautiful girl in my dreams,
I really am so in love with you.

Wesley Scott

Give to Receive

If Jesus lives within your heart
And peace is within your mind,
Then you have found the rock
Some seek but never seem to find.

There is no other door to open;
There is no other way;
I am the way, the truth, the light
Are the words that Jesus did say.

I guess what seems so strange to those
Who have given the Lord our heart,
Is that some do not yet understand
That giving is simply the very first part.

If we give our lives to Jesus,
Immortal then shall we be;
For Jesus gives us back new lives
That will last throughout eternity.

Eternal through the blood of Jesus,
Christians shall all someday stand;
They shall sing praise to the king of kings,
Who shall rule throughout the land.

Giving to God

God loved David for his obedience;
Abraham and Noah, for the faith they did show;
Jacob, for his determination and perseverance;
And us, for the trust that we come to know.

He opens our hearts to His forgiveness
And offers us the seeds we wish to sow;
His promise to us is He will always be near;
He will guide us faithfully wherever we go.

As we give of ourselves freely, gladly and willing,
We can feel honored it was us that He chose
To help spread His gospel to every nation,
And to be the open door that no one can close.

Let love and obedience flow from our hearts;
Let His light through us so brightly shine;
Out of the darkness, sinners are guided to Him,
Through the faith-filled prayers of yours and mine.

Wesley Scott

Going Home

He is now safe in his heavenly home;
His lifetime here on earth is through;
He is now among old friends,
As one day, he will be again with you.

He was a blessing to all who knew him;
A true friend to whom you could turn;
A man who had a deep, caring spirit,
Whose heart was full of love and concern.

Words can't convey the pain you must feel,
As we too all feel a deep loss inside;
He blessed our lives for many years;
The door of his heart was always open wide.

His memory will live on here among us;
Fine stories at times we can share;
We know, in our hearts, he's in heaven,
Emerged forever in his Father's care.

A Good Deal

It seems everyone is looking for a good deal;
Well, here is a great deal for you;
You can get in on the very best thing there is;
It's been around since the sky has been blue.

The price is so very reasonable;
In fact, would you believe it's free?
Yes, I will bet you your bottom dollar,
It's the very best deal you will ever see.

You can trade in your body for a new one
That has an unlimited mileage guarantee;
Plus, all the services it will ever need
Are thrown in as a bonus - and still all free.

So, when your old one gets all worn out
From the chuckholes it hits on life's way,
There is a new one ready and waiting;
And, as I said before, there's nothing to pay.

You have got to be willing to trade it
After it has gone its very last mile;
But the peace it will bring is everlasting,
Forever and ever - not just for awhile.

I bet you wonder what I am talking about;
Well, I can't say I blame you if you do;
If you will just give your life to Jesus,
You will see every last word is true.

Wesley Scott

Good Morning Holy Spirit

Good morning, Holy Spirit, how I love you;
I am so glad you are walking with me today;
You give me strength I know I can depend on,
    Strength in everything I do or say.

You are the standard my heart strives for,
The very spirit of my God who dwells in me;
You are the buckle of my life and salvation,
The spirit of my Lord who has set me free.

Help me that my life brings honor this day
To my heavenly Father to whom I owe all;
Help my heart to be open and responsive,
That I may answer when I hear you call.

Thank you for your patience, Holy Spirit;
You are considerate in everything You do;
Help me to bridle my tongue and my mind
    So my focus will stay more on You.

Grace of God

The grace of God is our perfect Lord Jesus,
For without Him, no grace would there be;
It is His righteousness that covers our sins,
So that acceptable to God, the Father, are we.

He is our provision in all aspects of life,
And, without Him, there is nothing at all;
He is the light that shines through darkness
And causes the blindness in our eyes to fall.

We have so many human shortcomings
For which Jesus does fill in the gap;
Truly, He is our fulfillment in life;
He redeems us from the enemy's trap.

We thank you, Father, for such a great gift,
The sweet grace you give through Your Son;
Our hearts are overflowing with gratitude
For all the wonderful works You have done.

Wesley Scott

Greatness of God's Love

Nothing overshadows the greatness of God's love;
    We should share it with others we know;
    Then like tiny seeds that are placed about,
        In the field of love, they will grow.

God's love is so deep and yet gentle and strong;
    He's always there with an outstretched hand;
    He waits for us to reach out and receive,
So, in His righteousness, we can forever stand.

We are bound by His love with everlasting bonds,
    Though the ties themselves we cannot see;
    We can feel them pulling on our hearts,
    Drawing us ever closer to Him continually.

May God's spirit of forgiveness and love
    Be ever present in us each day;
    May we always reflect the glory of God,
    In our lives, through what we do and say.

The greatness of your love, oh our Father,
    Our human minds cannot comprehend;
    By faith alone, we are guided by Your ways;
We are bathed in the love You constantly send.

Growing in Faith

No one is born full of faith,
It is a growing to be done from within;
It comes from trusting our God
And living a life not full of sin.

So fertile is the garden of our heart,
That it will grow any seed that is sown;
Unless the seed we plant is faith,
Confusion and doubt may soon be known.

Look to Him, and trust on His Word,
Let your faith in Him continually grow;
Give Him credit for the good things of life
That He in His goodness has let us know.

Trust in Him for little things,
Then be watchful as they come true;
Soon, there will be a mountain of faith
That will dwell inside of you.

Let our focus be on our Lord,
As walking hand in hand are we;
As we draw closer to Him daily,
The more transformed our lives will be.

Wesley Scott

Happy New Year

As we enter into the new year God has given,
Let's be firmly committed to do our best;
To make our lives more unto His liking,
A better year now than all the rest.

We should be forgiving, as we aren't perfect,
And we shouldn't expect others to be;
If we are eager and willing to learn,
A much better year, I know it will be.

Let's wake up each day with a new vision,
Happy, willing and eager to go,
With a heart full of love, gladly to give,
And encouraging words anxious to sow.

Have a hand ready to reach out and help
Someone having trouble on their way,
To encourage, support and do all we can;
Thus, helping them have a better day.

May our reaching out be a start this year,
A small glimpse of how it will be
When Jesus is crowned victor of all,
And He lives forever with you and me.

I Must Go Now

Like a mighty ship on an ocean of blue,
I must now set sail for ports anew.

Try not to cry when I am gone,
For me, there awaits a brand new dawn.

Someday, I will see you again once more
In a brand new world, on a faraway shore.

My journey on this earth is through,
The cargo I carry is sweet memories of you.

I must go now, the tide is high;
It is my time to say good bye.

Wesley Scott

Idols and Money

From all the gifts God gave to them,
A golden calf they had made;
They worshiped it instead of God,
To Whom all honor should be paid.

We know it is sin what they did
In those days of so long ago;
Yet, a closer look we should take
At this life we now live and know.

Has money become the god of our life?
Does it lead our own lives astray?
Is the money some choose to worship,
The same as the golden calf of yesterday?

It is the will of our heavenly Father
That our worship be to Him alone;
Let us turn from earthly praise
And cast our hearts before His throne.

In the Fullness

In the fullness of Your love, I am walking;
In the fullness of Your grace, I stand today;
In the fullness of Your mercy, I now receive
The healing that You give to me this day.

In the fullness of Your death, I gained salvation,
For I know, sweet Jesus, You did die for me;
I accept Your precious blood that has cleansed me
And from bondage, forever more, has set me free.

In the fullness of the stripes, You suffered,
When they beat you, my Lord, unmercifully;
It was for healing I may now know within me,
And that I may share in Your total victory.

In the fullness of His love, our God did raise You;
He set You free so that death would be no more;
By Your stripes, You did bring healing to my body,
And by Your rising, You did open heaven's door.

In the fullness of my love, I now offer
All to you, dear Lord, that I can be;
I accept all these truths into my life,
Everything You did, was done with love for me.

Wesley Scott

Jesus

The prophets announced His coming;
A star did show the way;
The angels took the shepherds to Him
That wonderful, glorious day.

He did walk upon the water;
He did calm the stormy sea;
He healed hundreds of the lame,
And He made the blind to see.

He fed five thousand in the desert
With one basket of fish and bread;
He called Lazarus forth from the grave
And gave him back life instead.

He came into the sinful world
To cause all of us to see;
He alone is the way through life;
He will guide us into eternity.

The sun did hide its face
When they crucified Him that day;
Three days later, He ascended into heaven
In a beautiful, magnificent way.

I am the way, the light and the truth
Are the words that Jesus did say;
You have to ask Him into your heart,
There is no other way.

I cannot possibly doubt
That what He said is true;
I know the reason that He came
Was for the salvation of me and you.

Higher Thoughts

Jesus Touched Me

Jesus touched my heart
And a tenderness entered me;
A tenderness hard to explain,
Yet forever in me it shall be.

A tenderness born of peace,
I feel within my soul;
A tenderness so complete,
My being does feel whole.

In special love, He enters in
When we do claim His name;
His seal is set upon our soul,
And we will never be the same.

As believers, we're set aside
From the others of the world;
We are wrapped in Jesus' banner
Until the day it is unfurled.

Tis then that He will say,
"Come and enter in with Me,
Into My Father's kingdom,
To the place I built for thee."

Wesley Scott

Joyous Christmas

The glory of God has descended this day;
In His great love, He has blessed the earth,
He has given to us His only begotten Son,
And today we celebrate His glorious birth.

He came not in a kingly fashion,
As so many thought He would;
So they welcomed not this gift,
Who was bringing with Him only the good.

The angels came down from heaven
To welcome in the new-born king;
Their heavenly voices sang praises to God
For the salvation He did bring.

Let our voices echo the singing of the angels,
As, with happy hearts, we celebrate this day;
We give thanks to God for His most holy gift
That time can never take away.

If you listen with a grateful heart,
You can still hear the angels sing,
Peace on this earth, goodwill toward men,
All praise and glory to the new-born king.

Look Forward in Faith

Look forward to the answer you seek in God
And not to the problem about which you pray;
Step forward in faith, and lift up your hands;
Start giving thanks to God, start this very day.

He is the dream maker that forever will be;
In His Word, He pledges His love to you;
All that He has, He offers so freely,
So, reach out in faith and receive as you do.

He has defeated the power of our enemy;
The battle was fought, was won, and is through;
When the victor's crown was set on His head,
He said, "Come my friend, and I will share with you."

Nothing is stronger than the command of God,
For His strength shall forever remain;
He will answer you according to His will,
He declares in His word many times over again.

Wesley Scott

The Man Inside

There is a man that dwells inside,
Neither flesh nor bone is he;
Behold, he is the spirit man
That the Father gave to me.

He expresses himself out through me;
He is the conscious I hold inside;
His life in me is very sacred,
For my destiny on Him does ride.

The spirit is created to live forever,
Our body is made to return to dust;
This is the will of our great creator,
Who is always right, holy and just.

Our physical body is but for a season,
An expression to the world outside,
Who sometimes judges us on what it sees
And not what is dwelling deep inside.

Ours are the eyes that see the world,
The spirit man beckons us to see above;
We should take the blinders off our eyes,
And see all things as He does in love.

Higher Thoughts

Merciful Father

Help us, Lord, to be open to change,
So the veil of darkness can be taken away;
We can then find our total liberty in Christ,
As we draw nearer to Him with each passing day.

The Lord is so great, and He is mighty too;
His mercies overshadow all He does do;
As we yield to Him our sinful hearts,
He joins them to His and makes them new.

Aren't you glad His heart is full of grace,
And He considers not the wrongs we have done?
He removes them as far as the east is from the west
When we place our trust in His precious Son.

We have all sinned and fallen short of His glory,
Yet His love for us always remains strong;
His heart overflows with richness and mercy;
He sees us as Jesus, with no hint of wrong.

Oh, merciful Father, maker of all things,
We humble our hearts and offer them to You;
Help us to be obedient to Your Word,
And always put You first in all that we do.

Wesley Scott

Missing You

How my arms have longed to hold you
And feel your sweet body pressed to mine;
I want to gaze into your beautiful eyes,
To me, you are always so heavenly divine.

I have missed the sweetness of your lips
And the soft, loving touch of your hand;
In my heart, there will never be another
Anywhere in this great, mighty land.

My ears have longed for your sweet laugh;
It makes me feel so very good;
You have found your way into my heart,
Just like I knew you always would.

I know I have told you I love you
Hundreds and hundreds of times before;
My love for you keeps growing deeper,
It seems every day, I love you more.

You are the most wonderful part of my life,
I wouldn't want it any other way;
What more can I do to show you my love,
My sweet angel, you just have to say.

I know I am a very blessed man,
Who God, in His goodness, created to be;
For the most beautiful woman God ever made,
He wrapped her in love, and He gave her to me.

Money and Happiness

How much happiness can money buy?
How many tears can it stop when you cry?
How many heartaches can it pay?
How many memories can it wash away?

How much sunlight can it bring to you?
How many friends that will remain true?
Can it restore a friendship faded away?
Can it bring happiness into each day?

How many smiles to lips can it bring
At what may seem a silly thing?
Can it buy love, which should be free?
Can it bring peace between you and me?

Can it cause the spirit within to rise?
Can it provide a big surprise?
Can it take back one unkind word
That you wish someone had not heard?

The answers to the questions above are no,
Because money can come, and it can go;
Instead, you should search deep in your heart,
Talking to Jesus is a good place to start.

Wesley Scott

Mothers

I give thanks to God for mothers,
He so graciously caused there to be,
Untarnished with the passing of time,
Always encouraging, no fault do they see.

God surely made mothers with hearts of gold,
With the patience and love to forebear
The often trying times of raising children
Which he so lovingly places in their care.

A mother is a friend you can always depend on,
No matter what happens, she won't turn away;
She has faith in her heart to believe in you,
Regardless of the things others may say.

Because there lies so deep within her
The compassion and caring God has stored,
A mother is often the anointed one
Who does lead her children to the Lord.

There is a special love I hold in my heart,
One of the most cherished possessions to me
Is the love a mother has for her children,
No deeper earthly love can there be.

Mountains in Our Life

When the mountains in our life seem so big
That there is just no way to get around,
We should not forget the power of our wonderful God,
For through Him, all answers are found.

God is the answer, there is no other way,
For in all things, He promises to see us through;
So rise up, oh spirit of faith in our hearts,
For, through faith, God will provide for you.

He delivered Job from ashes to riches,
Provided the sacrifice to replace Abraham's son;
Through the scriptures, His provisions are astounding;
He is Jehova Rapha, the all-providing one.

Say be gone to the mountains in Jesus' name,
Use the power He has given from on high;
You can overcome all things through Him;
He promises you victory when, in faith, you try.

Wesley Scott

Mr. Uptight

If I give an inch, I'll have to give a mile
I once heard a blind man say;
Not blind in his eyes, but blind in his heart,
For it really doesn't work that way.

As you give, so shall it be given unto you
Is the way that Jesus taught;
And it's the way it actually works,
In life, you will experience that a lot.

Rigid is not the grass on the prairie
That the gusty winds do blow,
Yet they stand so tall and straight,
For great flexibility, they do know.

If we bend, we will not break,
For God didn't make us that way;
And it isn't going to hurt Mr. Uptight
If things don't go exactly his way.

It's better to give then to receive
May sound like an old cliché,
But its reason for being lies in the Bible,
And the Bible is the truest book today.

My Angel from Heaven

Oh beautiful maiden, the fairest of all,
From what part of heaven are you?
I know that's where you must be from
To affect my heart like you do.

Tell me, are you really an angel?
That's what I'd surely like to know;
I feel in my heart that you are,
I just want you to say that it's so.

What is it like up there in heaven?
Is everyone as beautiful as you?
Why were you sent down to earth?
What makes me love you like I do?

How come your smile makes me feel so good?
And your glance takes my breath away?
When I look into your eyes, I see love,
One that consumes me both night and day.

Do you know I am in love with you?
Yes, you have stolen my heart away;
Oh, my beautiful angel from heaven,
It seems I love you more each day.

Wesley Scott

My Heart and You

My heart is full of the love I have for you,
In my mind, it never fades away;
Your beautiful image I see before me,
Every moment of each new passing day.

The joy my heart knows when you are near
Brings feelings I have not known before;
It makes me feel a little closer to heaven,
As my heart within me does joyfully soar.

In my dreams, I reach out and touch you;
I hold you close and never let you go;
The feelings of love burn so deep within me,
And these wonderful thoughts continue to grow.

My heart feels lonely when I am not with you,
An emptiness that just won't go away;
My feelings of love grow stronger and stronger,
They are deeply ingrained and forever to stay.

My Special Love

The song in my heart sings of a sweet love,
The most special love I have ever known;
For God, in his goodness, has joined us together,
So we will have each other and not be alone.

There is a special song that plays in my heart,
The beautiful music is created by you;
You are the most important part of my life,
And you stay on my mind whatever I do.

How pretty you look in the flickering light,
Just like an angel that God sent to me;
My heart is enraptured by the deep love I feel,
Always in your presence is where I want to be.

He has bound us together and caused deep love;
The feelings I have grow stronger each day;
The longer I know you, the more I do love you;
I want to be with you every step of life's way.

Wesley Scott

New Beginnings

Be proud of yourself and your accomplishments;
You have stayed the course and won;
As you step out now into the world,
A new chapter of your life has just begun.

There are many cross roads in this world
Where a decision must be made by you;
Trust in God, and believe in yourself,
And pray for guidance in whatever you do.

Where God leads, surely He will provide;
If you ask, He will make the path straight;
Love God deeply, and talk to Him often,
Always seek His will, and on Him, you can wait.

May the pathways you choose be joyful,
And bring happiness and contentment to you;
May your life be enriched in many ways;
May fulfillment dwell in all that you do.

One Day at a Time

God only gives us one day at a time,
He never promised us more;
So, we should make the most of it,
And see what it holds in store.

Live your life to the fullest,
As each day were the last;
Always look towards the future,
And don't get hung up in the past.

Keep a smile upon your face
And happiness in your heart,
And all the worries of yesterday
Very soon from you will depart.

Treat each person as your friend,
Even though they may not be;
Hold no hatred in your heart,
No pangs of jealousy.

Start each day with life anew,
A treasure to behold;
And God, in all His goodness,
Will enrich you a hundred fold.

Wesley Scott

One with Him

Jesus encourages us when we are weary;
He understands the problems we know;
He is the essence of all good things,
And His love to us, He does show.

He gives us courage when we are weak;
He is the strength on which we stand;
He is the one who rules our hearts,
And one day, He will rule the land.

He has created everything that is
And all that will ever come to be;
He is the master and the king,
And we the captives He has set free.

Our freedom lies within the Lord,
If in faith we have claimed His name;
Then, we can be one with Him,
One and all the same.

Our Thoughts

Let us not dwell on the wrongs in our life
Or the addictions that hold us there;
They should be far away from our thoughts,
So it can be the mind of Christ we share.

Does not our anger lead to resentment?
And resentment to a hardened heart?
Forgiveness is always kept far away
When hatred is free to play its part.

If we forgive ourselves and others,
The roots of bitterness will cease to grow;
Our mind will then find new fulfillment,
Where contentment and love are ours to know.

So, let's be careful of the seeds we sow,
And select each one with love and care;
Our minds will then be full of godly things,
Because our thoughts have put them there.

Wesley Scott

Palm Sunday

Hosanna was the song they sang
To Christ that glorious day,
As He rode triumphantly into Jerusalem
He fulfilled what the prophets did say.

Palm branches lined the street He rode,
As they laid them before His donkey's feet;
With much joy, thanksgiving and honor
Did the people their Savior greet.

Here was the king that God had promised;
Surely, their salvation did lie at hand;
Much was the joy and singing that day
Throughout all of the entire land.

But Jesus did carry a heavy burden,
Which no one else could possibly see;
He knew this was the end of His journey,
The time to fulfill His holy destiny.

He knew their joy would soon become anger;
And, as prophesied, they would cut Him down,
For He was the perfect lamb of God
Riding in the streets of this holy town.

Participation

Christianity is not a spectator sport,
Participation is the name of the game;
We're all born equal in the eyes of God;
He sees each of us exactly the same.

We are the precious jewels in His eyes,
Bathed in the righteousness of His Son;
In His presence, we are all worthy,
Yes, each and every one.

"Go ye forth into all the world,"
Are the words that Jesus did say;
He instructed no one to be a spectator,
But encouraged us all to play.

We are part of His Holy Spirit,
And one day it will fill the world;
Jesus will come in all His glory,
And the flag of peace will be unfurled.

So, be encouraged to participate
As we live in this world today;
With Jesus being on our side,
There is no reason for any delay.

Wesley Scott

Pathway of Life

On the pathway of life, there once stood
A man alone, desperate and confused;
The friends which he had known
Disappeared, after him they had used.

Deep was despair and great was darkness;
It sought to consume his whole mind;
He was ready to let go and give up,
And leave his lost life far behind.

Anguish and bitterness were in his heart,
For no hope he had to share;
Then God caused a man to cross his path,
Who deep in his heart did care.

He ministered in love to the wounds so deep,
And, ever so slowly, they began to heal;
Little by little, with encouragement,
A bond between them did seal.

He led this man to Jesus, his Savior,
And set his feet on the way;
He taught him to love and how to forgive;
He also taught him how to pray.

There now walks a man on the pathway of life,
With deep purpose within his soul;
Not broken anymore, but born of the Lord,
For Jesus had made him whole.

He tells the story to all who will listen,
And it is said, that many now do;
Of how, when you are out and so down trodden,
All of the things Jesus can do for you.

Higher Thoughts

He now pastors a church in a little town,
And there, I believe, he will always be;
There is also an elder in this church -
The man who taught him to see.

Wesley Scott

Patience and Trust

If patience knows the depths of our heart,
Our anxiety will then fade away;
Then trust will become a deeper part
For the cares we face each day.

Patience is a form of trust
In our Father's will for our lives;
And impatience is the fruit of distrust,
Upon which our deadly enemy thrives.

Patience can't find lodging in our heart
If trust does not already dwell there;
They are the fruit of the same tree
From which God would have us share.

We are like clay in the potter's hands,
And He wants us to follow His ways;
So trust must be a part of our lives,
And patience should fill our days.

If we make patience a part of us
As we abide in His holy will,
Then our God, the father of love,
Our every need, He will surely fulfill.

Peace Within

In the stillness of the night,
He whispers in my ear
Words of comfort to me,
That I should have no fear.

He calms the stormy sea
That churns within my heart;
Peaceful waters fill my soul,
And my troubles soon depart.

I'm so glad I trust in Him,
He sends the answer to my prayer;
He is the friend on whom I can depend,
And I know He's always there.

How shallow life would be,
If I knew not of His love;
All the blessings of this life
Are sent by my Father up above.

Oh, thank you, Jesus, for all You've done,
You have won the battle for me;
You have given me victory over all,
And, with joy, I offer my heart to Thee.

Wesley Scott

A Perfect Mother

God gave each of us a perfect mother,
A perfect one for you, and a perfect one for me;
Then God placed a love in their hearts,
A love so strong, that forever it shall be.

He knew which mother would guide us best
And watch over us with tender loving care;
The mother that God gave to us,
Is the most perfect mother from anywhere.

She would sit up with us all night,
If sickness would ever come our way;
She would rock us gently in her arms,
As silently to God, she did pray.

She rejoiced with us in our victories,
No matter how small they may be;
They seemed as important to her,
As they were important to you and me.

God has called some mothers back to heaven,
Like angels, they watch from above;
They seek to guide us from all harm
And honor God's eternal stamp of love.

Perfect through God

He knows all of our transgressions,
Yet no fault in us does He see;
We are cleansed by the precious blood
Of our Savior who has set us free.

Perfect we stand before Him,
Yes, perfect in every detail;
For the covering of Jesus is over us,
And righteousness is our veil.

The holiness of Jesus surrounds us,
And His spirit does dwell inside;
He has joined us unto Himself as one,
As the groom does take his bride.

The heavenly halls of the holy city
Do know the sound of each name;
They're entered in the lamb's book of life,
And forever there, they shall remain.

His covering shall always be upon us;
His righteousness to claim as our own;
Undaunted, we can enter the presence of God,
To worship before His holy throne.

Wesley Scott

Plant the Seed

God intermingles our lives, that's easy to see;
Brothers and sisters of each other,
We are created to be.

We are part of the body and must do our part,
To lift each other up with the love
God has placed in our heart.

Our body must function with one goal in sight,
To bring honor to Jesus,
For He is the light.

Together we are one, in this our strength lies;
We must encourage each other
And strengthen our ties.

We must share our lives, for how else can we see
The work our Father has destined,
For you and for me.

If we do not plant the seed, it cannot grow;
Then how will others see the light,
The One we want them to know?

The fields are fertile, and the time is here,
So we should plant the seed now,
The ending draws near.

Look for someone in your path today,
One that God just happened
To have walked your way.

Power through Jesus

Don't base life on your past failures
And give them power over your days to bind;
Instead, look out beyond your shortcomings,
And, in God's grace, new strength you will find.

He, alone, is the power that enables us,
In Him, is met our utmost desires;
His is the hand that always upholds us,
His is the love that never tires.

All our wrongdoings, though many they may be,
The blood of Jesus has washed them away;
Now we can stand and praise Him joyfully,
Pure and holy before Him, in every way.

What wonderful days we look forward to,
Precious times of knowing only victory;
His is the power that overcomes all things,
And He gives this power, willingly and free.

Rise up in our hearts, oh spirit of faith,
For we seek to be like Jesus in every way;
The first step we take upon this path,
Is to move out in faith and start today.

Wesley Scott

Praising the Lord

All praise to Jesus, our blessed Redeemer,
He has defeated death and set us free;
Broken are the bonds that held us tightly,
He has turned darkness into glorious victory.

All glory to the Father, for He has sent Jesus;
Worship God, He is faithful in all He does do;
He has given eternal life to His children;
All followers of Jesus, praise God, it's true.

Lift up your hands, and praise our Redeemer,
Let joy pour forth from our hearts today;
Jesus has bridged the gap to the Father,
He has taken the vast veil of darkness away.

Let our mouths sing songs unto Jesus,
With overflowing joy, He lives today;
He alone is the perfect, spotless lamb;
He opens the door and shows us the way.

Precious Memories

Deeply sealed within my heart
Are precious memories of you;
One by one, I call them forth
And relive them all in review.

There is wonderful magic in each one,
They are so precious in my mind;
I guard them with my intense love,
Finer memories, I will never find.

Each one is sealed with your face,
Which I see before me all the time;
You are the inspiration in my heart,
The reason I set these words to rhyme.

May we share our earthly lives
Forever, until the end of time;
May we build more precious memories,
Ones that will never be left behind.

Wesley Scott

The Prize

Absolutely free, nothing to buy,
These are the words that caught my eye;
Everyone is eligible, a winner guaranteed,
The poster I saw went on to read.

Winners' names written in a large book,
At this I must have a closer look;
Promised not to be a computer printout,
Wow, what can this contest be all about?

All the below prizes guaranteed for free,
Hey, this is really the one for me;
Rent free for life, all utilities paid,
In the most beautiful place ever made.

Wow, this contest is boggling my mind,
Sure doesn't seem like those other kind;
Life abundant and health forever more,
I wonder who put this poster in the store?

There's got to be a catch, it can't all be free,
No one is going to give that much to me;
Life everlasting, all dreams come true,
How can they promise that to me and you?

All of the above, guaranteed in writing,
This is getting even more exciting;
I just have to get to the bottom line,
I need an entry blank I can sign.

I recognized the name on the bottom line,
And a conviction came to this heart of mine;
Yes, all of the above is so very true,
Jesus gave it to me, and He'll give it to you.

Higher Thoughts

Promises of God

When we wrap ourselves in the promises of God,
With conviction in our hearts that His word is true,
Then contentment will dwell within our inner self,
And the feeling of assurance is born anew.

For, surely, He leads us into green pastures,
Where the peaceful waters always await;
He is the good shepherd as He watches over us,
And He, alone, is the keeper of the gate.

He guards over the promises He has made,
To see they are fulfilled in every way;
'My words shall not return void unto Me,'
Are the words of promise God did say.

Let's keep His word locked deep in our hearts,
And know fulfillment in Him there will be;
Jesus is our assurance and precious redeemer;
It's the promise He made to you and me.

Wesley Scott

Putting Faith into Action

To each has been given a measure of faith,
It is a free gift from God's holy hand;
What we do with this God-given faith,
Determines how we will live in this land.

As we water our faith with the word of God,
Surely it will grow and become very strong;
His word is life and breath unto us,
If we live by it, we can overcome all wrong.

When we act on our faith, it is pleasing to God,
The more we use it, the more He does give,
Until we can speak the desires of our heart
And bring them into reality, as we live.

Always strive to remain strong in your faith,
Hold tight to the truth of his holy Word;
Tell others all the things you believe,
Give praise to God, and let your joy be heard.

Quality Time

We should give good quality time
To the Lord whom we love and serve;
For, truly, we know deep in our hearts,
Quality time, He does surely deserve.

All that we are, we owe unto Him,
Our body, spirit, soul and mind;
He should never be taken for granted,
Never left standing back behind.

As we put Him above everything in life,
And honor Him always, as it should be;
Then, quality time is what we are giving,
The kind He desires from you and me.

He owns every day He gives us,
Each moment is another gift for free;
All that is His, He provides unto us,
The very best there can possibly be.

Wesley Scott

Remembering Jesus

Jesus gave His life that we may live
More abundantly in every way;
This we celebrate with holy communion
We share together on this day.

Eternal salvation was the gift He gave
When He died upon Calvary's tree;
All of the agony that He suffered,
Was done for both you and me.

The grave had no power over Him,
As triumphantly, He rose from the dead;
Death had bruised our Savior's heel,
But He had crushed its head.

As we lift our bread and wine today
And celebrate everything Jesus has done,
Let thanksgiving reign within our hearts,
For together in Him, we are one.

Revival

Revival will come once more to this land
When we, the children, truly believe
We can do all things God says we can
And, in our faith, reach out and receive.

We shall take what He has promised
And boldly accept His Word as true;
The power of God will then be shown,
As He magnifies Himself through me and you.

He is our strength, and His spirit is within us;
We should be yielding to His calling today;
He should be first in our hearts and minds,
And the desires of idolatry should be cast away.

We should be full of faith, not linger in doubt,
And never give unbelief a foothold to grow;
That will be the time, within our midst,
A new-born revival is what we will know.

Yes, revival must first start in our hearts,
Then, in deep faith, we reach for His hand;
He will give all the blessings we can hold,
It is then that revival will fill this land.

Wesley Scott

Rewards of Labor

My pleasure comes from doing the will of My Father
And finishing the work He sent me to do;
This is the spiritual food you don't know about,
But it's the reason I was sent by the Father to you.

Vast fields of human souls are ripening all around
And are now ready for the harvest of today;
The reapers shall be paid the richest of wages
And shall share with the sowers in eternal pay.

What a great joy awaits both the sower and reaper,
For they drink of the living water flowing from Me;
They shall pitch their tents and live side by side,
By the river of life running through eternity.

I am the good shepherd, and they are My sheep,
They do the work of the Father I have sent their way;
The rewards they receive will be eternally lasting,
For they labor on My behalf this very day.

Robes of Righteousness

The robes I had were as of rags
To wear before the throne;
Then Jesus gave me His own robes,
So I could wear them as my own.

Now, as I stand before the Father,
To worship and to pray,
He sees me as His dear Son, Jesus,
Righteous in every way.

I thank Jesus for the robes He gave,
Even though they don't belong to me;
Jesus earned them with His blood,
As He hung on the cross at Calvary.

It is by His grace that I now stand,
Not by my own power and might;
I am a sinner, but God forgives me
And makes me righteous in His sight.

Wesley Scott

Safely Home

Safe in the arms of Jesus
Your loved one is today,
There, everlasting in His care,
Forever more, he will stay.

In your heart, there is a yearning
For things as they were before,
All the wonderful times you shared
Before he was called to heaven's door.

If your loved one could speak to you,
These words I feel he would say,
"Rejoice with me in this new life I have,
I can't wait to share it with you one day.

Our precious Lord is so beautiful,
And now I can see him face to face;
Millions of years it would take to tell
Of this wonderful, glorious place."

Seasons of My Life

The winter of my life was cold and lonely,
Yet, I knew of not a better way to be;
I sought comfort from this earth and all its riches;
I sought all the things the world could give to me.

Deep in my heart, there was this longing
For the fuller things of life I could not find;
Though the world blessed me with its kindness,
Somehow, I was always looking back behind.

I was searching for a meaning for my life,
That somehow there just never seemed to be;
I knew one day the seasons would be over,
And wondered then, what would become of me?

Then springtime filled my life when I met Jesus,
Flowers bloomed, and the storm clouds passed away;
In my life, there dawned a feeling of fulfillment
That I had never known upon a winter day.

The buds of life within my heart started to grow,
Swollen by the soft and gentle rain;
The more my heart was exposed to His purpose,
The more I realized what joy I had to gain.

The summer of my life was so refreshing,
A time of growing ever closer to my Lord;
A time to learn and understand more deeply,
The abundance of peace my Savior had restored.

Now, my heart is full and overflowing,
It ripples in the soft winds fall does bring;
It's filled up with the fruit He has planted,
Listen to the joy with which my heart does sing.

Wesley Scott

Seek Me

Seek Me with your heart, and you will find Me,
For it is My desire to grow even nearer to you;
I gave My only Son for your salvation,
The greatest sacrifice I could ever do.

I ask only that you will love Me truly,
And put no other god upon My throne;
For I, alone, am God, the great creator,
Come, share with Me in everything I own.

In your heart, you must see I am the mighty one;
I created all things as far as your eyes can see,
From the highest of the twinkling stars
To the depths of the mighty, roaring sea.

This earthly life lasts but for a moment,
And once it is gone, it shall not return;
Trust Me, for the moment is passing,
And your future is My deepest concern.

I am sad when you are not near Me,
My children, I love you one and all;
Draw close to Me, and I will comfort you,
Please, open your heart and hear My call.

Self-Love

Only to the extent that we love ourselves,
Can our appreciation for others be shown;
Yet, the love we have is meant to be shared
And not held back, aloof and alone.

We all know our faults so very well,
They are sometimes all that we see;
We then get caught up in bitter emotions
And prohibit our love from flowing free.

As we give, so shall we receive
Encircles the lives we now live;
But, often the part that's hardest is,
It's our own selves that we must forgive.

Repent from the mistakes in your life,
Lay them aside, and let them be;
Unleash the love that is within you,
Allow it to flow, abandoned and free.

Wesley Scott

The Sensitive Servant

He was more sensitive to the needs of others
Than He was to those of His own;
He said I have come as a servant,
For this reason, He left the throne.

He came to bring peace to the souls of men,
Where there had never been any before;
He came to show the way to the Father,
The oneness again, He would restore.

Let us all try to be good servants,
And conduct our lives each day
So others may know, by the love we show,
That we are trying to follow His way.

He lives in us, and He gives to us
So much love we can never repay;
Caring for others brings joy to His heart;
May He help us be more sensitive today.

Shadows of the Past

The shadows of the past are behind us,
God has put them many miles away;
He has taken them from His remembrance
Is what His holy Word of truth does say.

So why dig around in earthly graves
For faults that are no longer around?
He has made us righteous in Christ
And put our feet on solid ground.

We have been called to a brand-new life,
Not one that is soiled and torn;
A life perfect through our Lord Jesus,
For into His family, we have been born.

Let's humble our hearts in thankfulness,
Be mindful of His mercy and grace;
We should always depend on His strength
And meet our future face to face.

Step out of the shadows of the past,
For it holds no condemnation for you;
Focus on your future with Jesus,
And let Him guide you in all you do.

Wesley Scott

Sin

Sin is a deadly disease of the mind,
And like a cancer, it seeks to grow;
It can overcome all of our thoughts,
Until complete victory it does know.

The fruit it bears is the fruit of evil,
And evil itself seeks to destroy;
It robs from us the glory of life,
The happiness, laughter and joy.

It causes despair to rise in our hearts
And depression it brings for free;
It strives to overcome the light within,
Which our God has placed in you and me.

Live in the light the Lord has provided;
Don't let the shadows of sin dim your view;
Jesus is the light which surrounds us,
And He has brought victory with Him too.

Spirit of God

The spirit of God is a small quiet voice
That speaks in the stillness of your mind,
It tells you of God's perfect will
And how a closer walk you can find.

Your heart should be silent in prayer,
And ask the Holy Spirit to speak to you;
The concerns you carry within you,
Are the same concerns God feels too.

If you don't listen, then how can you hear
What the Holy Spirit is trying to say?
How will you be able to discern His will,
If you don't listen when you pray?

As you open yourself to His will and ways,
His blessings can pour out through you;
Everlasting goodness He holds in abundance
When you put Him first in all you do.

Listen with your ears to the call of His voice;
Make it your desire to know what He does say;
Open your heart when He knocks on the door,
And prepare for Him a lovely place to stay.

Wesley Scott

The Spoken Word

We are just what we say we are,
No more or no less shall we ever be;
The power of the spoken word
Turns the wheels on the road of destiny.

Let us speak words that are only good,
And leave all of the unkind words behind;
Always be loving and caring to others,
For the spoken word has the power to bind.

It can join us together as a strong union,
Or it can tear us apart in utter despair;
Mighty are the words from our tongues,
So be sure to use them with utmost care.

Our Father is God, the great creator,
Who spoke into existence all that we see;
He gave us His own Holy Spirit and power,
To guide us into what He wants us to be.

Let us speak forth in the power of His Word,
And call on the precious name of the Lord;
Use His name that is above all names,
For through Him, all things are restored.

Stepping Stone

Let me be a stepping stone
To help my brother rise,
That he may be a blessing
Before Thy holy eyes.

Help me, Lord, to lift him up
With everything I say;
To encourage him in all things,
To be a friend in every way.

Grant that I not forsake him
If trouble should arise;
Help me to remind him of Your strength
And not be the one to criticize.

Help me, Father, in all I do
When I lift my brother to Thee;
I want to be a good servant,
Lord, as faithful as You are to me.

Help me, Lord, to open my heart
To the things he has to say;
Help him to become more like You
In every single way.

Wesley Scott

Submit to Christ

We can't do it in our own,
That's mighty plain to see;
We get things so botched up
In this world of you and me.

People fight among themselves,
And nations do the same;
Seems like once it's started,
It's just an endless game.

Who will be king of the mountain?
And who will pull him down?
It's the senseless contest we play,
For centuries, it's been going around.

If we all submit our hearts to Christ,
And put Him on our throne,
All the bickering would finally stop
And no weapons would we need to own.

What a day to look forward to,
When peace will rule the world;
Christ will live once more on earth
With His flag of peace unfurled.

Sunset

God reflects His glory
In the setting of the sun each day,
That no artist brush could ever match
Nor mankind take away.

How glorious is the sky He paints,
With the blending of each hue;
The Master creates it new each night
To signal that the day is through.

The beautiful colors are blending now,
Turning mostly to a deeper red;
I love to watch the sky each night
As God puts the sun to bed.

In the stillness of the evening,
At the closing of the day,
If you just listen with your heart,
Maybe you will hear Him say:

"Rest yourselves, My children,
Restore yourselves anew;
In the morning, I will put the sun
Again in the sky for you."

Wesley Scott

Surrendering

The more we surrender our hearts to the Lord,
The more we can feel His spirit working within;
It speaks to us of trusting and faith in God,
To the goodness of love and absence of sin.

We can feel the depth of His caring,
The wooing of His spirit reaches our ear;
It speaks to our hearts of total surrender
And a complete letting go of all our fear.

The spirit of the Lord lives in our hearts,
All of His gifts He wants us to know;
If we totally surrender all that we are,
More of His goodness, we let Him show.

Hold not onto things of this earthly world,
Seek His treasures, and He will give them to you;
They are patiently waiting within your grasp,
This is what His spirit urges us to do.

Teaching Overtime

Hungry are the hearts God has placed around you;
We watch not the hands of the clock upon the wall;
We thoroughly enjoy your expounding of the Word,
With which He has blessed you, in the richness of His call.

You open up our hearts as furrows in a field,
Plowed, cultivated and ready to sow;
In richness and wealth, we long for the seed,
Each word of God you so deeply know.

You speak of trials and sorrows you have known,
You open your heart so we may see
That our God is faithful in all He does;
You are such a blessing to followers like me.

I come to be fed and am not turned away hungry,
I can drink contently to my fill;
I absorb the word God gives through you,
As I pray in my heart, He always will.

If you become discouraged, just look around
At the happiness in the faces you see;
It's put there in part by your readiness to serve
And feed the people God caused there to be.

You speak encouragement to my heart
And bring peace to my restless mind;
As I bask fully in the goodness of His Word,
All thoughts of the clock are left far behind.

Wesley Scott

Thorn Bush & the Flower

There was a thorn bush that grew by the wayside,
Then one day, a beautiful flower it did see;
It prayed with all of his heart and might,
"Lord, please give that beautiful flower to me."

The Lord said, "Though you are but a thorn bush,
I will give the very lovely flower to you."
He then caused the wind to blow in a seed,
Which He watered with the sweet, morning dew.

Now, a pretty flower so sweetly grows
In the briar patch where I still stand;
A beautiful flower sent from heaven,
And not one planted by a human hand.

With my briars, I shall protect her,
I shall surround her with all my love;
Because this flower from heaven
Was sent to me by my Father above.

I am the thorn bush in this story,
And you the beautiful flower that grew;
All of my life, I shall spend entwined
Around sweet, wonderful, beautiful you.

Thy Cup Runneth Over

Honor your God with your entire spirit,
With your whole mind, and all of your will;
And the wonder you will feel in your heart
Will surely cause it to overfill.

It will spill out the joys of the Lord,
For all of His love, it cannot contain;
You will have plenty to share with others,
And millions of blessings will still remain.

He holds the world in the palm of His hand,
The whole universe is in His control;
Oh, how we should honor the maker of all,
The redeemer and comforter of our soul.

Fall in love with the God you serve,
And give credit where credit is due;
Offer back the life He has given,
Freely out of His love just for you.

The cup of your heart will overflow,
So much love does He give in return;
The joy you feel being close to Him
Kindles the fire of praise, forever to burn.

Wesley Scott

Thy Word

Help me that when I read Thy holy Word,
I capture it deeply, unending inside;
Help me to hide it close in the folds of my heart,
Where Thy Holy Spirit in me does abide.

Held me to understand the truths I read,
Which you have given by Your holy will;
Cause worldly anxieties to cease inside,
And bade my heart be humble and still.

Cause me to become as the finest of screens
That when thy holy Word passes through,
All of Thy truths, I truly do glean,
As in my spirit, I so want to do.

May I regard each precious word given
As the finest of all treasures to behold;
Let it bind my spirit and heart to Thine,
In the strength You know, in depths yet untold.

Grant unto me a far deeper understanding
Than I have ever known in my heart before;
Cause there in me a desire never ending,
That will hunger for Thee forever more.

Place Thy tenderness deep in my heart,
So I am sensitive to Thy holy will;
When Thy spirit beckons, I will follow,
And I can drink of Thy goodness until my fill.

Cause there to burn a light so bright,
That to Thy glory, it shines clear to see;
Let each day I walk be according to Thy will,
Father, this is my fervent prayer to Thee.

Higher Thoughts

Two-Way Street

Life is like a two-way street,
We can go whichever way we choose;
One way leads to happiness,
The other way causes us to lose.

Why should we wander back and forth
Upon this street where we now live,
When, deep within our hearts, we know
The promise each way does hold and give?

We should focus only on the good,
It makes us feel so wonderful inside;
It brings peace within our heart and soul
If we are open to receive, with nothing to hide.

We were created by God to enjoy this life,
So we should always try our very best;
Then the road on which we travel
Will never become a failing test.

There is no struggle we can't overcome;
Through Christ, we have the strength inside;
As we travel along this two-way street,
Let's always be sure, we are on the right side.

Wesley Scott

Unbound

There are no shackles that hold us
Bound to where we are;
We set the limits within our minds,
And then we go just that far.

Faith in our Savior does enable us
To expand the capabilities we know;
It is the will of our heavenly Father
That His children be allowed to grow.

If Jesus is the strength within us,
There shouldn't be any bounds to know;
His power is the greatest of all,
And His spirit through us does flow.

Let's look beyond the limits we set
And toss all of them away;
Use them as markers on the road,
That say Jesus did pass this way.

Unforgiveness

If you hold unforgiveness within your heart,
What good does it really do?
And who is this feeling actually hurting?
Why, usually nobody but you.

If tension fills your mind,
Then there is no peace in your heart;
You really can't enjoy yourself
When unforgiveness is playing its part.

If you hold anger within your heart,
Then how are you to rationalize;
Yet, much less, forgive the other
Who was wrong within your eyes?

Forgiveness is the key to peace within,
So anger the lock itself must be;
You should unlock the gate to your heart
And set the feelings of love in you free.

As you forgive, so you are forgiven,
This the Bible does plainly say;
If you are to follow the ways of Christ,
You should throw all of your anger away.

Wesley Scott

Unkept Promises

Unkept promises line the road
To heartache and despair;
Bitter memories they have sown,
They grow abundantly everywhere.

Perhaps, a promise should not be made
Unless we know it can be kept;
A promise is better off unsaid
Than a river of bitter tears being wept.

Heartbreak can come in many ways,
But an unkept promise is the hardest of all;
When a promise is given in trust,
It hurts so much when the trust does fall.

Through our faith, we trust in Christ,
And in the promises He did give;
He will never betray our trust
And triumphant in Him, we do live.

We need to be willing to forgive others
During this our earthly stay;
And, on that day, when Jesus comes again,
He will take all of our hurts away.

Vision

Without a vision, our confidence will perish;
Vision brings hope for a better new day;
It causes greater fulfillment to enter our lives;
It draws us close to God in a special way.

When we have a vision, we don't wander about,
Filled with confusion or full of fear;
When we trust in God, and look towards Him,
Each day of life, our vision becomes more clear.

So, capture a vision and hold it inside,
Watch it grow more real to you each day;
Until, at last, your vision is fulfilled,
And you walk with Him in every way.

Let us make Christ the center of our lives,
And seek to honor Him in all that we do;
Can you hear the voice of our heavenly Father
Saying, "Yes, My child, this is My vision for you."

Wesley Scott

Walking in Faith

Seek to be righteous in all your ways
But, when you slip and fall,
Reach out and hold Jesus' hand;
He will always hear your call.

With stumbling blocks which Satan lays,
He tries to steal our trust;
But, if we are to follow Jesus' ways,
Overcome them all we must.

Jesus gives us the strength we need,
Our victories do all lie in Him;
He watches the path and encourages us
In times when our vision does grow dim.

When, at last, the other end
Of the path we finally see,
We will pass through heaven's door,
Into His arms eternally.

We will look back upon the path
That seemed so hard and straight;
We'll see it was really paved in love,
And that it led straight to heaven's gate.

Walking in the Spirit

Help me to walk in Thy spirit, dear Lord,
So I honor You in all that I do;
I want to grow stronger in my faith;
Each day, I want to depend more on You.

I long to feel a newness in my spirit,
Deeper than I have felt before;
Let Thy Holy Spirit flow through me,
Day after day, just a little bit more.

Help me to follow the light cast before me,
For Thy glory surely does ease the way;
Thy kindness shines brighter than diamonds;
You are so faithful to me each day.

Make known unto me Thy will for my life,
So I can live in service to You;
May I always be faithful in serving,
In all that I say and all that I do.

Open my heart to a deeper understanding,
As I put all wrong thoughts away;
Lead my footsteps close to Your side,
This from my heart, I do earnestly pray.

Wesley Scott

Wants and Needs

Do you get what you want and need from life,
Or is it simply passing you by?
Is happiness alive and sound in your heart,
Or is your well almost running dry?

Are you content with the life you live,
Or do you feel it's just a trap?
Do you flow with the things about you,
Or are you so tight, you could snap?

If we try to seek out happiness
From a world of personal gain,
The higher we get, the more it seems
That our quest is all in vain.

There is a fullness that forever remains
And never from you shall it depart;
That fullness comes through Jesus Christ
When you take Him, as Savior, into your heart.

We Want to See
(Matthew 21:30-34)

We want to see, said the two blind men,
Sitting along the road that day;
When Jesus moved and touched them,
Instantly, their blindness was taken away.

Are we not sometimes like the blind men
When our fulfillment we try to find
In a jumbled up world of broken dreams
That hatred and greed have so entwined?

They received their sight, arose and followed Him,
Giving glory and praise to His name;
Let's pray that Jesus lifts the veil from our eyes,
So that we can arise and do the same.

In Him, is our hope and salvation,
Though times in our walk we fail to see;
Jesus is the power within us,
And we are the captives He has set free.

Let the veil be lifted and taken away,
And, through Jesus, sight restored to our eyes;
For a mighty warrior now walks beside us,
Deep in our hearts let us fully realize.

He is the power that we stand on,
The miracle worker we serve day by day;
He is the strength that sustains us,
The one who takes our blindness away.

We thank you, Jesus, our precious Savior,
It's Your strength that will carry us home;
In Your name, we bind the power of darkness,
We seek to serve You, and You alone.

Wesley Scott

The Weaker Vessel
(1 Peter 3:7; Ephesians 5:25)

As we give, so also shall we receive,
Jesus so plainly and unmistakably did say;
The truth of these words lives in our minds,
A prophecy fulfilled in us each day.

For unless we do sow, we cannot reap,
And barren the fields of our hearts will be;
If nothing is planted, nothing comes forth,
It is the same with the weaker vessel and me.

God in His love has joined us together,
To complement each other in all we do;
I am to love her as Jesus loved the church,
Does this not speak deeply in your heart to you?

All that He had, our precious Lord did give
When He emptied himself for His only bride;
He lay down His life, His completeness before her,
That forever she could be close to His side.

Then I should give honor, I should give love,
Tender compassion should pour forth from me;
All that I am, I should offer unto her,
For she is the vessel God entrusted to me.

She will bloom in the showers of love
And enrich my life fully in measures untold;
The garden of my heart will flourish in abundance,
All of the harvest my heart will barely hold.

I will be enraptured by the depths of her love
As together we walk the pathway of life;
Fulfillment shall know the days God gives us,
What a wonderful vessel, my God-given wife.

Higher Thoughts

Who Is Jesus?

He is the light, the gateway of heaven,
The doorway which all must pass through;
The good shepherd who watches over us,
The all righteous, the one who is true.

He is the salvation who once lived among us,
The true bread of life for all mankind;
The Savior of all who gives eternal life,
That only through Him we can find.

He is the lamb, the anointed sacrifice,
The one who split the darkened veil;
He is King David's song of deliverance,
The one through whom we can prevail.

He is the vine that gives life to its branches,
Jacob's ladder on which we can climb;
The alpha, omega, the rock of salvation,
The holiest of holies, the maker of time.

He is the foundation, the truth of all ages,
The solid rock on which we can stand;
The king of my heart, the Lord of my life,
It is to Jesus, I stretch out my hand.

Wesley Scott

The Will of God

Question not the will of God,
For He is perfect in all He does do;
Though you may not understand why,
His will is always just right for you.

God sees beyond the shadows of tomorrow,
He understands all that happened yesterday;
He fits it all into a perfect picture
In the reality we live in each and every day.

When we humble our hearts to His understanding,
And not try to fit into all the earthly mind,
Peace and tranquility will flow through our lives,
Each new day, there will be a treasure to find.

God's wisdom surpasses all we know;
He spoke into existence everything we see;
We are His children, and He loves us dearly;
His will is perfect, just as it should be.

Higher Thoughts

Windows of My Mind

I was looking out the windows
On the backside of my mind,
I saw all of the places I had been
And the ones I had left behind.

Many things I would do differently
If I could do it over again once more
Is often the thought within my mind
As the old memories I do restore.

But why get lost in yesterday
When the future lies ahead?
The yesterdays have come and gone,
All but the memories are now dead.

Certainly, we can learn from our past
About how life's challenges can be met;
It makes the future that much clearer,
For the days that lie before us yet.

Don't get lost in your yesterdays,
The life we live is here and now;
It's the time to honor and serve our Lord
And do the very best we know how.

Wesley Scott

Witnesses in the World

When the love of God abides in us,
We must reach out from within;
We can prove to the world around us,
We are no longer the children of sin.

Good works He has set out before us,
Those that He would have us do;
With our lives, we can express
The goodness bestowed on me and you.

Our lives are to be as a mirror
And reflect His glory dwelling within;
He is embodied in us by His Holy Spirit,
Who convicts us to not walk in sin.

With our mouths, we are to praise Him,
While with our lives, we do His will;
Then to those around us, we may witness
The love and patience He does instill.

The unsaved can then be drawn to the Father,
And His spirit can speak to their heart;
Their lives they can then choose to surrender,
And of His kingdom can also be a part.

The love of the Lord is truly contagious,
It will affect all who are open to hear;
Let's give thanks to God for this privilege,
And witness to others while we are here.

World of Make-Believe

In the magical world of make believe
Where the elves and fairies play,
That's where our minds can easily wander
On a nice, warm, sunny day.

We can see all the little animals
Busy running to and fro;
They sing their happy, little songs,
As merrily about their way they go.

Everyone is talking about a party
In the meadow the farmer did mow;
Here comes a mouse, let's follow him,
And see where it is that he does go.

We followed a pathway through the forest,
Worn smooth by many little feet;
As we walked along, we sang a song,
As did everyone we happened to meet.

They were all dressed up in pretty clothes,
The variety of colors was amazing to see;
A green frog with a shiny, red vest
Hopped right over and said hello to me.

There were all kinds of animals everywhere,
With cloths spread neatly on the ground;
Their baskets were nearly running over,
Full of the tasty treats they had found.

They had acorns, sunflower seeds and pine nuts,
Strawberries, blueberries and gooseberries too;
Anything you would probably ever want,
And everyone was so happy to share with you.

Wesley Scott

They all said we're so glad to see you,
  We are just so happy you are here;
  We don't have parties all that often,
  Usually only just a few times a year.

A squirrel sat right down beside me
And offered me a piece of gooseberry pie;
  She said she baked it all by herself,
  Then said with a twinkle in her eye:

"We are having a baseball game this afternoon,
  And we would just love to have you play;
  We always have all kinds of fun,
  And it is such a warm and beautiful day."

Well, I agreed to play and told them so,
  But I warned them I wasn't too good;
  They looked at me in a funny sort of way,
  Then they laughed as hard as they could.

They said, "We don't really care who wins,
  In fact, no one even keeps score;
  We just go home with happy memories,
  That's all we really come here for."

They chose up sides and started to play,
  It was the funniest sight you ever did see;
  There was a big bear playing on first,
  The umpire was an eagle in a tree.

Second base was covered by a mother raccoon
  Who had two babies at her side;
  Shortstop was a kangaroo mouse,
  He could jump ten feet in just one stride.

Higher Thoughts

Playing third was a beaver with one, purple shoe
And a tail he drug on the ground;
They all thought his tail was a base,
So sometimes they chased him all around.

Playing in left field was a funny, little bird
Who wore a great big, yellow hat;
He said, "I can catch any ball you hit,
If I can just see where it is at."

Center field was played by a long-legged deer,
Who kept jumping still-legged on the ground;
In right field, was an amusing gopher,
Who kept waving his pink coat all around.

For balls, they were using acorns,
For a bat, a limb off a dead tree;
A muskrat was the first batter up,
He was as comical as he could be.

He kept making faces at the pitcher
And waving his bat in the air;
He had on blue, cowboy boots
And a bright, red feather in his hair.

The eagle umpire said, "Let's play ball,
But don't throw the ball at me;
I can't see what's going on
If I have to keep ducking behind the tree."

The pitcher was a long-legged jack rabbit
With his ears tied up in a bow;
He said this confuses everyone, as to
Just which way the ball will go.

Wesley Scott

He wound up and threw the ball,
It was the funniest thing to see;
Everyone was running all around
Wondering where that ball could be.

Then the rabbit took off his hat,
And there on the top of his head
Was the ball they were all looking for;
It all happened just like they said.

Then the eagle said, "I can see the sun,
It is slowly going behind the hill;
I believe it's time to end this game;
I think we'd agree, it gave us all a thrill."

The umpire made me a hat from a knot
That he found growing on a tree;
The rest all gave me a hug or two,
One couple even gave me three.

What a wonderful day we all had
In the meadow the farmer did mow;
We all promised to come there again
And put on another fun-filled show.

World-Driven Heart

I seek to overcome my world-driven heart,
And turn it over to my Lord and His ways;
Truly, I know in the depths of my spirit,
He wants only good in all of my days.

I strive to reach deeper into His abundance,
Which I know He wants to share with me;
My world-driven heart must be overcome,
If I am to be all He wants me to be.

He is the strength I know I can depend on,
Though yet often times fail I may;
He is my comforter, my life's biggest goal,
My hope above all that never fades away.

One day I will trade my world-driven heart,
And my dear Lord will make it brand-new;
No more will I wrestle with my old heart,
For that day, Jesus, I will be with you.

Wesley Scott

Worship

Worship the Lord with praise, oh my soul,
For love alone He came;
Rejoice, oh my heart, in the works He has done,
Sing praise to His glorious name.

Walk straight, oh my feet, in the ways of the Lord,
Be not tempted to wander astray;
For the Lord Jesus, Himself, did set the course,
And He promises to show the way.

Radiate, oh my life, the love of the Lord,
Glorify the works He has done;
Honor the life God freely does give,
And the blessings He shows through His Son.

Shine, oh my life, that others may see
The joy that I feel deep inside;
Speak, oh my mouth, of the glory of God,
Let go, oh my heart, open wide.

See, oh my eyes, the work to be done,
That I will honor His holy will;
Receive, oh my heart, all the love He gives,
Drink, oh my soul, to your fill.

Hear, oh my ears, the message of God,
Let me bury it deep in my heart;
Guide, oh my spirit, this life I live,
And from His path let me not depart.

The Wounded Soldier

Somewhere on the battleground, a wounded soldier lay,
Whose eyes would never again see the break of a new day;
He called not out for help, for he knew it would be in vain,
If he did, it probably would be to see a fellow soldier slain.

To comfort his soul, he prayed to his God,
But never once did he curse this far foreign sod;
As he lay on the cold ground on his own,
He thought of his loved ones back at home.

He prayed for their health, and that their spirit be brave,
When they were all told of his soldier's grave;
As his eyes glazed over, and they turned to the sky,
He laid still and alone, a brave man, not afraid to die.

Wesley Scott

CPSIA information can be obtained at www.ICGtesting.com
Printed in the USA
BVOW080036280912

301544BV00001B/6/P